THE
DAILY SPARK

180 easy-to-use lessons and class activities!

THE DAILY SPARK

Critical Thinking
Critical Writing
Great Books
Journal Writing
Math Word Problems
Poetry
Pre-Algebra
The SAT: English Test Prep
Shakespeare
Spanish
Spelling & Grammar
U.S. History
Vocabulary
Writing

THE
DAILY SPARK

Great Books

SPARK PUBLISHING

Spark Publishing
A Division of Barnes & Noble Publishing
120 Fifth Avenue, 8th Floor
New York, NY 10011
www.sparknotes.com

ISBN-13: 978-1-4114-9981-2
ISBN-10: 1-4114-9981-6

Please submit changes or report errors to www.sparknotes.com/errors.

Written by Ann Crowther.

Printed and bound in Canada.

Contents

Introduction

The *Daily Spark* series gives teachers an easy way to transform downtime into productive time. The 180 exercises—one for every day of the school year—will each take students five to ten minutes to complete and can be used at the beginning of class for inspiration or at the end of class to help clarify themes and ideas.

The exercises in this book may be photocopied and handed out to the class, projected as a transparency, or even read aloud. In addition to class time use, they can be assigned as homework exercises or extra-credit problems.

Use the *Great Books Daily Spark* to help your students understand and explore twenty of the most-popular works of English literature. Each exercise encourages critical thinking and creativity. Whether students are choosing between Tom Sawyer and Huck Finn, analyzing Holden Caulfield's hunting hat, or writing in Newspeak, they will be engaged with and interested in great literary works.

Spark your students' interest with the *Great Books Daily Spark*!

Life in Exile

In *The Scarlet Letter,* Hester Prynne exiles herself to the edge of her Puritan community after she is publicly shamed for the crime of adultery. For years, she lives on the outskirts of society, both physically and socially, because her peers generally scorn or shun her.

Imagine that your role in your community changes after you are punished for some sin or crime. You opt to reside at the edge of the community. Although you do business in the community, you are an "untouchable," as far as other citizens are concerned.

How would life as you know it change if you lived outside the structure of society? Write a paragraph about how being an "untouchable" would alter your behavior or your personality.

Shame on You

The Puritan community shames Hester Prynne as punishment for her crime of adultery. First, she must stand on the town scaffold while people ridicule her. Then she must wear a scarlet A on her breast as a badge of shame.

Imagine that your high school has adopted "shame sentences," which are handed down for breaking rules. Students caught outside of class without a pass, for example, must carry around a ten-pound wooden slab, and students who plagiarized are forced to wear a big yellow P.

Think of three other possible shame sentences for breaking various school rules. For each, explain why the punishment fits the crime.

Dimmesdale's Dilemma

Although Hester Prynne and Arthur Dimmesdale have committed the same crime of passion, they lead very different lives. Despite her shaming, Hester is mentally healthier than Dimmesdale, who tortures himself privately but refuses to confess. Some critics have suggested that Dimmesdale suffers more than Hester because he keeps his sins secret.

Consider Hawthorne's characterization of Dimmesdale. Based on the descriptions of the minister, do you think Dimmesdale would be happier if he confessed? Discuss why or why not in a short paragraph.

Fact or Fiction, Friend or Foe?

Numerous characters refer to a "Black Man" living in the forest. Does this Black Man really exist? What does it mean if he does?

Consider the following questions as you formulate your answers in a paragraph:

- Which characters are associated with the Black Man? Which characters are identified as his friends?

- Which of these identifications are just? Why?

- Does the Black Man really exist, or does he represent some kind of superstition or prejudice? If the latter, which superstition or prejudice?

I Love You, I Hate You

In the conclusion of the story, the narrator reflects on Roger Chillingworth's various misdeeds:

> It is a curious subject of observation and inquiry, whether hatred and love be not the same thing at bottom. Each, in its utmost development, supposes a high degree of intimacy and heart-knowledge; each renders one individual dependent for the food of his affections and spiritual life upon another; each leaves the passionate lover, or the no less passionate hater, forlorn and desolate by the withdrawal of his subject.

Is this assessment of human emotion true? Discuss why or why not in a short paragraph. Does *The Scarlet Letter* support the assertion above? Do your life experiences support it?

No More Secrets

Hawthorne's novel teaches us the dangers of keeping our "sins" secret. Recall a time when you kept secret something you did that was wrong or that hurt someone in some way. Write a paragraph in which you describe your "sin" and the effects of keeping the sin a secret.

Who Am I There?

When Hester Prynne and Arthur Dimmesdale meet in the forest, they are transformed into much "freer" people. Alone with each other, Hester and Dimmesdale hold hands, bestow caresses, and feel happier than they do in their usual, everyday lives.

Write a paragraph about a place that seems to alter your everyday attitude or personality. How does it change you?

Sick, Sick, Sick

According to some readers, Nathaniel Hawthorne's writing demonstrates the depravity of human nature. List as many specific examples as you can from *The Scarlet Letter* that suggest that human nature is fundamentally twisted or sick.

Can You Hear Me Now?

At the novel's end, Dimmesdale confesses. Yet nobody seems to understand or believe in his confession. Write a response from the point of view of a Puritan in Dimmesdale's community.

Trenchant Twain the Satirist

Mark Twain was a master satirist, and *The Adventures of Huckleberry Finn* is perhaps his funniest satire. In fact, the novel begins with this warning:

> PERSONS attempting to find a motive in this narrative will be prosecuted; persons attempting to find a moral in it will be banished; persons attempting to find a plot in it will be shot. *BY ORDER OF THE AUTHOR, Per G.G., Chief of Ordnance.*

Look up *satire* in the dictionary. Then define *satire* in your own words. Hint: Satires use irony, humor, and wit…. Once you're clear on the definition of the word, brainstorm as many examples as possible of other satires. Which movies take a satirical stance toward groups of people, trends, traditions, and so on? Which comedians are known for satirizing individuals, groups, lifestyles, etc.?

Yo, Huck. Whassup, Dude?

Twain uses a number of dialects throughout his novel, including various types of "southern speak." Here's an example from Chapter XVI:

"Pooty soon I'll be a-shout'n' for joy, en I'll say, it's all on accounts o' Huck; I's a free man, en I couldn't ever ben free ef it hadn' ben for Huck; Huck done it. Jim won't ever forgit you, Huck; you's de be' fren' Jim's ever had; en you's de ONLY fren' ole Jim's got now." I was paddling off, all in a sweat to tell on him; but when he says this, it seemed to kind of take the tuck all out of me. I went along slow then, and I war't right down certain whether I was glad I started or whether I war't. When I was fifty yards off, Jim says: "Dah you goes, de ole true Huck; de on'y white genlman dat ever kep' his promise to ole Jim."

Translate this passage or another passage from Twain's novel into your own words, using modern English. For a twist, try translating the passage into another contemporary dialect, like Valley Girl, Surfer Dude, or Emo Kid.

A Banned Book

Since Twain published his book in 1884, many schools and libraries have banned it on numerous occasions, for numerous reasons. Initially, some people felt that the book was too profane, and others claimed that it might inspire immoral behavior, especially in little boys. More recently, the controversy has been over the novel's depiction of Jim, which some have called racist.

What do you think? Write a paragraph about whether this novel should be banned by libraries or schools. Why or why not?

Tom or Huck?

Consider the characterization of Tom Sawyer in the novel. Then think about Huck's character. Would you rather be Tom or Huck? Why? Explain in a paragraph.

Blame Biology, Fault Society

Huck is quite a handful. Do you think his personality is a result of DNA and biology (nature)? Or do you think he was formed by socialization and education (nuture)? What about you? Are you the result of nature or nuture? Write a paragraph discussing your views.

Why Huck?

Write a paragraph about the point of view of Twain's novel. Why would Twain choose to tell the story in the voice of a virtually illiterate thirteen- or fourteen-year-old kid? What can Huck tell us that other characters cannot?

The Royalty on the River

They lie, they cheat, they steal. And Huck lets them get away with it—that is, until they go too far. **Just what are the duke and the king doing in this novel? Are they merely there to provide comic relief, or is there more to their presence? Explain.**

'Scaping the Sivilized Life

In the end, Huck decides to run off again, because he can't bear the idea of being "sivilized." Do you think Huck will succeed in escaping civilization? **Discuss why or why not in a short paragraph.** If Huck were living today, what would he have to do to escape twenty-first-century civilization? Where would he have to go?

Writing Under the Influence

Ernest Hemingway once remarked that all American literature since *The Adventures of Huckleberry Finn* owed a debt to that novel. Imagine that you're a famous writer about to publish the Great American Novel. Which aspects of Twain's book might you play with or emulate in your own book?

What a Mess!

J. D. Salinger drops hints that Holden Caulfield is unstable, not to mention unreliable, as a narrator. What do you think? Make a list of clues about Holden's troubled state. Is he a typical teen, or does he have other issues beyond the usual stuff?

Teens Behaving Badly

When *The Catcher in the Rye* first came out in the early 1950s, readers were shocked by Holden Caufield's character. He didn't act, speak, or think in ways that were considered appropriate for proper young men in postwar America. Decades later, troubled or rule-breaking adolescents are no longer news; in fact, such characters in fiction, in movies, or on television have become somewhat trite.

Make a list of real-life teen behavior that you think would qualify as shocking or controversial nowadays. In what ways are your examples similar or dissimilar to the fictional behavior of Holden Caulfield?

Holden's Hat

[Ackley] took another look at my hat…. "Up home we wear a hat like that to shoot deer in, for Chrissake," he said. "That's a deer shooting hat."

"Like hell it is." I took it off and looked at it. I sort of closed one eye, like I was taking aim at it. "This is a people shooting hat," I said. "I shoot people in this hat." (Chapter 3)

What do you think the hunting hat symbolizes? Write a paragraph about what the passage reveals about Holden Caulfield.

Holden's Savior Complex

Holden Caulfield believes that children need to be protected and that their innocence needs preserving. Phoebe, Holden's sister, challenges this idea with her independence and thoughtfulness. She seems able to see that her brother needs help and protection more than she does.

How much protecting and rescuing do kids really need? Write a paragraph about what kids need protection from. What can they handle knowing about and dealing with?

Holden All Grown Up

Imagine that twenty years have passed since the events Holden Caulfield narrates in the novel. Who has he become? What is he doing? Has he become a writer and recluse like J. D. Salinger? Or is he something altogether different? Has he become a phony? Write a paragraph about the grown-up Holden.

A Meaning in Time

At the end of the novel, Holden Caulfield reveals that he spent time in a sanitarium, but he chooses not to reveal the circumstances of his breakdown or cure. In other words, the end of the novel takes place prior to Holden's narration of the entire story. Does the language in this section, viewed alongside the language used elsewhere in the novel, indicate that Holden has matured or recovered? Is he ready to deal with people at an honest, personal level? **Discuss why or why not in a short paragraph.**

Phonies

Throughout the novel, Holden Caulfield rails against "phonies." How would Holden define a "phony"? What type of behavior typifies phonies? According to his definition, is Holden a phony? Are you?

Meet Jane Gallagher

Throughout the events Holden Caulfield relates in the novel, he seems fixated on the idea of a girl he knows named Jane Gallagher.

Exactly what does Holden remember about Jane? Why do you think she is so important to him? What do his feelings for Jane tell you about Holden? Write a paragraph about Holden and Jane.

Holden at the Museum

The best thing, though, in that museum was that everything always stayed right where it was. Nobody'd move…. Nobody'd be different. The only thing that would be different would be you. (Chapter 16)

Holden Caulfield reflects on the lack of change at the museum. He can understand and appreciate the never-changing, frozen museum world. But he fears and feels anxious about the way *he* has changed from museum visit to museum visit.

Write a paragraph about a place that you visit now and again, such as a vacation spot, an old neighborhood hangout, or a relative's home. Does returning to the same place force you to notice changes in yourself, as it does for Holden? Does the realization of change make you happy? Or, like Holden, are you troubled by change?

Reinvent Yourself

Jay Gatsby totally reinvents himself. Imagine that as you go off to college, you decide to change your name and to alter large portions of your personal history. Who do you become?

Tell your new story in a short paragraph—but retain at least one true detail from your past.

The Real Deal

What does Jay Gatsby feel for Daisy? Is it really love? Why or why not? How do you know? Write a paragraph about Jay and Daisy.

The Elegant and the Quirky

In *The Great Gatsby*, F. Scott Fitzgerald creates some rather elegant characters—and some quirky ones.

Of all the characters in *The Great Gatsby*, whom do you think you'd most enjoy meeting for lunch? With which character do you have the most in common? Write a paragraph in which you explain whom you would want to hang out with and what you'd discuss.

The Great Gatsby

Double Standard

In *The Great Gatsby*, Tom and Daisy Buchanan's marriage is ruled by a double standard. Tom feels that he is free to engage in extramarital affairs, but he is outraged at the thought that his wife might get involved with someone else.

Double standards are fairly common in families, in relationships, and even in social institutions. Frequently, what seems to be good for one person is not allowed for another.

Make a list of double standards you have experienced or observed. Are they connected in any way? Does there seem to be a logical reason behind any of them, or are they all the result of irrational prejudice?

Humans, the Masters of Illusion

F. Scott Fitzgerald seems to create two Gatsbys: the legendary, aloof party thrower, who is all elegance and polish, and the lovesick innocent, who is willing to gamble everything on a hopeless dream of love.

In real life and in fiction, we often encounter people who harbor secret selves. Discuss an experience with a person or a fictional character who, like Gatsby, turned out to be something other than what he or she initially seemed to be.

A Mother's Hope

In Chapter I of *The Great Gatsby,* Daisy discusses her hopes for her daughter. She remarks:

> "I hope she'll be a fool—that's the best thing a girl can be in this world, a beautiful little fool."

What does Daisy's remark about her infant daughter tell you about Daisy's own character? What does it tell you about society in 1922, the year the novel takes place? Write out your thoughts in a short paragraph.

Dreaming the American Dream

At the end of *The Great Gatsby*, F. Scott Fitzgerald suggests that the American Dream has shifted from its original ideal of "the pursuit of happiness" to a materialistic pursuit of wealth.

Do you agree? Is the American Dream now just a matter of money? A combination of money and happiness? Or does the dream depend on the person?

Symbols

In *The Great Gatsby*, Fitzgerald places a great emphasis on our use of symbols, or the significance we place on the objects and people in our lives. For example, to Gatsby, the green light at the end of the Buchanans' dock, and even Daisy herself, stand for his dream of recreating his happy times with Daisy in Louisville five years ago. To another man, this green light and this woman might be meaningless.

Which objects or individuals hold particular significance for you? Make a list and discuss what each object or individual represents for you.

The Women of *The Great Gatsby*

In real life, F. Scott Fitzgerald had to work hard, amass a fortune, and throw himself into a glamorous social world in order to win the hand of his socialite wife, Zelda. This experience, as well as his difficult marriage with Zelda (who eventually suffered a nervous breakdown), probably complicated his attitude toward women.

Discuss the attitude toward women in *The Great Gatsby* in a paragraph or essay. As you try to establish your argument about women in the novel, closely examine the behavior of the female characters and think about how the narrator, Nick Carraway, describes them. You might also consider the behavior and attitudes of the various male characters toward the female characters. How do the men treat the women?

What if History Never Happened?

In *1984*, Winston Smith's job is to alter historical documents to suit the needs of the ruling Party of his fictional nation, Oceania. The Party alters history and memories to cement its totalitarian control over the people of Oceania.

Consider the importance of history. Why do we study it in school? List one event in history that you think is essential knowledge. How would life be different had this event never happened?

Is Big Brother Watching You?

George Orwell's novel was intended to warn readers about the horrible possibility of totalitarianism at its most extreme. Make a list of which aspects of the novel seem to have come true in the decades since Orwell published it in 1949. Which aspects are, in your opinion, coming true in the twenty-first century?

The Walls Have Eyes

In *1984*, Big Brother is the official national leader and Party head. His face is everywhere, plastered on posters that scream,

"BIG BROTHER IS WATCHING YOU."

Big Brother's warm and friendly name is meant to reassure people. Yet Winston finds him troubling. Why? Make a list of details from the novel that can you cite to explain what makes Big Brother and his leadership so disturbing.

Because the Party Says So

Chapter I of Book One lists the Party's official slogans, which are inscribed in massive letters on the Ministry of Truth:

WAR IS PEACE

FREEDOM IS SLAVERY

IGNORANCE IS STRENGTH

How might these be true or untrue in the real world? Respond to each of these slogans with a few sentences.

Poverty + Decay = Trouble

The urban universe of *1984* is a mess. Big Brother's London is full of crumbling buildings with broken elevators and unreliable utilities. Meanwhile, hungry, impoverished Proles (proletariat people, or common workers) are everywhere.

These details are symptomatic of a totalitarian government. What details do you think would suggest that the government of Oceania was doing a good job? Write a paragraph that describes a stable, positive society. Be sure to include lots of details.

Life of the Party

Winston struggles to recapture his memories and his sense of life before the Party took over. Write a paragraph about how Winston tries to recover his past. What actions does he undertake to try to remember? Why doesn't his lover, Julia, do something similar as part of her own rebellion against the Party?

I Speak Newspeak

In the world of *1984*, Party members speak Newspeak, a language based on English but which contains far fewer words. For example, Newspeakers would say "ungood," rather than "bad," and "doubleplusungood," rather than "extremely bad." The Party wants to rid language of all nuances and shades of meaning in order to prevent antigovernment sentiment from entering the minds of the population of Oceania. In fact, "thoughtcrime," or the thinking of seditious, anti-Party thoughts, is punishable by torture.

Using George Orwell's essay on Newspeak (the Appendix to most editions of *1984*) and examples from the novel itself, write a paragraph in Newspeak about life in your school. Then translate your paragraph into Oldspeak, or the Newspeak term for "modern English."

Doublethink

The Party uses "doublethink," or the ability to maintain two contradictory ideas in one's head simultaneously and to believe them both to be true, in order to brainwash the population of Oceania.

Give a few examples of doublethink that you recall from the novel. How does doublethink help the Party to gain and maintain control of Oceania?

I Fear, Therefore...?

Throughout George Orwell's novel, Winston seems certain that the Party is watching and checking up on him at every turn. He approaches life with the fatalistic attitude that his capture by the Party is inevitable.

What's the connection between paranoia and fatalism? In a paragraph, discuss the connection between Winston's attitude and his ultimate downfall.

This Book Lights My Fire

In *Fahrenheit 451*, Captain Beatty, the fire chief, explains that books came to be banned and, ultimately, burned to avoid offending anyone. Reading simply became too offensive and too dangerous for common consumption.

Think about Captain Beatty's explanation for the book fires. Can a book really offend? How? When? Why? Can a book be dangerous? Discuss why or why not in a paragraph.

Curious Connections

Guy Montag is disturbed by his neighbor Clarisse because she leads him into personal conversations, because she is unlike anyone he ever has met, and because he feels unusually connected to her.

Have you ever felt super-connected to someone very different from you? How did you meet? Did you talk, or did you just feel linked from afar? Write a paragraph in which you discuss what happened.

I Can't Get No Dissatisfaction

People are prevented from deep, meaningful thoughts or relationships in Ray Bradbury's novel. Make a list of specific details about various characters in *Fahrenheit 451* that stand as signs that people are unhappy or dissatisfied with their vapid world. How do those signs express unhappiness and dissatisfaction?

I'm Not That Guy—or Am I?

Despite the popularity of book clubs, most people in the United States prefer watching television to reading. Is our society in danger of becoming like the one in which Guy Montag lives?

Answer the following questions three times: first from your point of view, then from Guy Montag's point of view, and, finally, from the point of view of your school's librarian. Are you more like Guy or more like the librarian?

- How often do you go for walks in nature?
- How often do you reflect on or question the way things are?
- How often do you read?
- Are you comfortable with the idea of a world without books or deep thinking?

Mark Your Territory by Doing Good

After Guy Montag joins Granger and his group, Granger tells Montag of his idea about the relationship between people and good works: according to Granger, when people think and work deliberately to change even a small part of the world, they leave behind some of their souls.

What will you do to leave your mark on the world? How? Why? Organize your thoughts into a paragraph.

Relationship Malfunctions

Mildred Montag seems to feel more strongly about her television parlor families than about her husband. Why do you suppose this happens in the Montag household?

What other relationships break down in the course of the novel? Make a list of relationship malfunctions in the novel.

Fahrenheit 451

Bradbury's Doublethink

In "Burning Bright," Guy Montag confesses to Professor Faber that he has gone around his entire life doing one thing while feeling something totally different. Even watching television coverage of his escape and chase fascinates him: although he has revolted against society, he still is concerned with appearances.

When have you felt ambivalence like Montag? Write a paragraph about a time when you felt two contrasting emotions simultaneously or when you felt one thing but did something else.

Why We Do the Things We Do

Forced to burn down his own house, Guy Montag ends up burning Captain Beatty, the fire chief, as well.

Write a paragraph about what prompts this action. Was it extreme, or was it warranted? Why?

Why Ecclesiastes?

Ray Bradbury's novel is full of allusions to and quotations from various works of literature.

List as many of the texts referenced by *Fahrenheit 451* as you can. Choose one or two with which you are familiar and discuss why you think they were chosen by Bradbury. What purpose do they serve in the novel?

Text and More Text

In *Frankenstein*, Mary Shelley created a novel that seems obsessively full of different types of texts, as well as the acts of reading and writing. The novel begins with the letters of Robert Walton, which include the life story of Victor Frankenstein. And Frankenstein's story includes the story of the monster, which itself includes the monster's struggle to learn to read.

Pick a story or text in *Frankenstein* and discuss its relationship to the novel's plot. How does this story or text fit in with the other stories and texts?

The Same but Different

Victor Frankenstein tells his tragic story to Robert Walton, who has saved him after he fell weak and ill from chasing the monster. Walton serves as a **foil** to Frankenstein's character—that is, by contrast, Walton highlights some of Frankenstein's important characteristics. But there are also striking similarities between the two characters.

List the similarities and differences between Walton and Frankenstein. Then comment on which characteristics are repulsive and which are attractive.

The Law of Change

At its core, *Frankenstein* is the story of Victor Frankenstein—how he grows, how he changes, and how he dooms himself.

How does Frankenstein change during the course of the novel? Write a paragraph about Frankenstein's evolution. What lessons can we draw from Frankenstein's character?

The Making of a Monster

Based on his physical description alone, Mary Shelley's monster would be a frightening sight. But more than his appearance makes this monster a monster.

Which characteristics make the monster of the novel monstrous? Using examples from the novel, how would you define a monster? Could any of the other characters be considered monsters as well? Write a paragraph about *Frankenstein*'s monsters.

Did I Ask to Be Born?

Did I request thee, Maker, from my clay
To mould me Man, did I solicit thee
From darkness to promote me?

Mary Shelley takes the epigraph of her novel from John Milton's *Paradise Lost* (Book X, 743–745).

Write a paragraph about how these lines connect to the monster's experience and emotions throughout *Frankenstein.*

Too Many Thoughts, Too Much Thinking

In many ways, *Frankenstein* seems to be a cautionary tale about the dangers of thinking and knowing too much or of seeking and using too much information, especially in the context of science. Might *Frankenstein* be a warning?

Do you agree that knowledge can be harmful or dangerous? Which types of knowledge? In what circumstances? Explain yourself in a short paragraph.

Pick a Narrator, Any Narrator

Frankenstein is rather peculiar: at one time or another, it has three different narrators.

Evaluate the three narrators. Whose voice do you prefer? Whom do you trust the most? Whom do you trust the least? Whom would you want to narrate your life story? Why?

Once Upon a Time ... Boo!

According to literary legend, Mary Shelley wrote *Frankenstein* while on vacation in Switzerland with her future husband, Percy Bysshe Shelley, and their friend Lord Byron in 1816. To pass the time, Byron proposed that everyone at the villa write a ghost story. Mary Shelley based her story on a vision she'd had.

Imagine that you were on hand for Byron's contest and write your own scary short story or scene.

Communing with Nature

On the brink of suicide, Victor Frankenstein wanders into the valley of Chamounix in Chapter 9. The beauty of the scenery cheers him, and his melancholy passes.

Explore the relationships between the characters of the novel and nature. Are the characters' links to nature genuine, or are they ironic? Explain in a paragraph or two.

Faced with Hardship....

The Grapes of Wrath dramatically, yet realistically, portrays the devastation of the Great Depression for the farm families of the Dust Bowl. These families were forced to move to California in the hopes of scraping by. Those who experience such hard times are forced to change their identities, roles, and lives in countless ways. Similarly, society must also change to accommodate the difficult circumstances and new identities of its members.

How does hardship or tragedy force individuals, families, institutions, and governments to change? Take your examples from the novel or from the real world and write a paragraph about hardship.

Rose of Sharon

Critics often note that Rose of Sharon's character is compiled from stereotypes and doesn't seem to fit with the realistic characters most often described by John Steinbeck.

Write a paragraph about how Rose of Sharon's character is special or different from the other characters. Why would Steinbeck want to set her apart from the others? How does her role become important dramatically as the novel comes to a close?

The Turtle and the Grapes

Some readers find it surprising, even irritating, that the third chapter of *The Grapes of Wrath* tells the story of a turtle's journey across an Oklahoma highway.

Why would John Steinbeck choose to tell the turtle's story? Discuss the relationship between the turtle's story and the rest of the novel in a paragraph or two.

A Billion Points of Light

The character of Jim Casy suggests that individual lives are meaningless unless individuals contribute in some way to the greater community.

Based on your experience, would you agree? Do you have to contribute for your life to have meaning? Write a paragraph in which you discuss the individual's responsibility to the larger community.

Fiction, Nonfiction, Fiction, Nonfiction, and So On

The structure of *The Grapes of Wrath* is unique. John Steinbeck alternates between chapters focused on the story and struggles of the Joad family and chapters that serve almost as reportage, discussing the common suffering of countless families like the Joads during the Great Depression.

What are the effects of the alternating chapter structure employed by Steinbeck? Write a paragraph about the advantages and disadvantages of structuring a novel in this way.

California's Promised Land

John Steinbeck portrays a California in which opportunists take advantage of one another. He notes, for example, that the state's farm communities of the 1930s were run by squatters—people who stole the land from Mexicans.

What's the relationship between Steinbeck's observations and the poor treatment received by the Joads and other migrants? Why might the California landowners react the way they do? What's the threat posed by the masses of new migrants? Explain your thoughts in a paragraph or two.

Pa Joad's Decline

Over the course of the novel, Pa Joad transforms. He begins as a strong father figure, a leader who carefully plans the journey to California and who works hard to protect his family. Over time, however, the hardships faced by the Joads wear Pa out. He withdraws, retreating inward and gradually breaking down. As a result, Ma Joad must find new, nontraditional ways to keep the family together.

Write a paragraph about Pa Joad's decline. What does his deterioration suggest about the impact of the Great Depression or of similarly monumental hardships on even the strongest of people?

Carpe Some

At the start of *The Grapes of Wrath* Tom Joad focuses on the present as a means of coping with his own uncertain life. However, his contact with Jim Casy transforms him, and he becomes fixated on the future.

Are you focused more on the present or the future? Is your motto "*carpe diem*" (seize the day) or "spend some, save some"? Write a paragraph about your outlook on life.

The Boss Rocks Tom Joad

Tom Joad transforms into a future-minded, responsible leader. To reassure his mother, he explains that his spirit will live on no matter what happens to him:

"Wherever they's a fight so hungry people can eat, I'll be there. Wherever they's a cop beatin' up a guy, I'll be there. If Casy knowed, why, I'll be in the way guys yell when they're mad an'—I'll be in the way kids laugh when they're hungry n' they know supper's ready. An' when our folks eat the stuff they raise an' live in the houses they build—why, I'll be there."

Musician Bruce Springsteen made a record called *The Ghost of Tom Joad*. Write a paragraph about why you think the idea of Tom's spirit would be important to an artist like Springsteen, who has long been known as a champion of the American worker.

Pip or Miss Havisham?

Over the course of his writing career, Charles Dickens created more than 13,000 characters. Which character in *Great Expectations* do you find most appealing or striking? Write a paragraph about the character you like best.

Dreams of the Unattainable

Early on in *Great Expectations*, Pip falls in love with Estella, even though she treats him callously and cruelly. Although Estella is beautiful, much of her appeal comes from her wealth, which makes her unattainable for Pip.

People often aspire to achieve or acquire things simply because they seem unattainable. Write a paragraph about a time when you or someone you know sought something or someone that appeared out of reach. What happened? Explain.

A Tale of Two Pips

As an adult, Pip tells his story. This means, essentially, that there are two Pips: Pip the character, who goes through various stages of development, and Pip the narrator, whose perspective is that of a mature grownup, reflecting back on his past. The elder Pip can thus poke fun at the younger Pip, even as he describes the feelings and experiences of his youth.

The split between the mature narrator and the immature character can be difficult to understand. To help clarify matters, think of a story from your childhood, preferably from when you were very young. Tell the story from the viewpoint of your teenage self reflecting on events from your early childhood.

A Life in 500+ Pages

Great Expectations is a **bildungsroman**, a story that chronicles the spiritual, moral, psychological, or social growth of a character, usually from a young person into an adult.

Think about Pip's growth from an immature boy to a mature man. Which realizations or characteristics distinguish the older Pip from the younger Pip? Write a paragraph about who or what changes him.

Great Expectations

A Novel Society

Charles Dickens portrayed whole societies throughout his novels—from the very wealthy to the very poor, from the educated to the uneducated, from urbanites to country dwellers.

Whom does Dickens seem to favor? Which class does he portray more sympathetically? Why? How do you know? Defend your position with examples.

Victorian Visions of Justice

Charles Dickens populates *Great Expectations* with diverse, multifaceted characters from both sides of the law. Within the novel, the good often suffer bitterly, whereas the bad often go unpunished. Why? What might Dickens be saying about law, justice, and morality in nineteenth-century England? Discuss your views in a short paragraph.

New and Improved?

In the original ending of *Great Expectations*, Estella remarries a country doctor after Drummle's death. One day, Pip and Estella meet and shake hands, and Pip notes that suffering seems to have taught Estella to understand "what my heart used to be." But Charles Dickens changed the ending into the happy, romantic conclusion we read today.

Critics have conflicting opinions about which ending is more appropriate for the story. Which do you prefer, and why? Organize your thoughts into a paragraph.

The Circumstantial Chasm

In Chapter 27, Joe bids farewell to Pip, now a wealthy gentleman, after an awkward meeting. Joe isn't upset about the uncomfortable atmosphere of their meeting, which he credits to their differing situations in life:

> "Pip, dear old chap, life is made of ever so many partings welded together, as I may say, and one man's a blacksmith, and one's a whitesmith, and one's a goldsmith, and one's a coppersmith. Divisions among such must come, and must be met as they come."

Think about a time when circumstances divided you from an old friend. Did you chalk your discomfort up to fate, as Joe does? Or did you try to overcome the circumstances and make the relationship work? **Write a paragraph discussing what happened.**

Miss Havisham's Satis House

Charles Dickens carefully describes Satis House and its denizen, Miss Havisham. Compare the two descriptions in a paragraph or two. How are they connected or similar? Which adjectives are used to depict the house, and which the woman? What's the relationship between person and place?

Certainly Uncertain

In Act II, Hamlet makes a speech about the wonder of human understanding:

> "What a piece of work is a man! How noble in reason, how infinite in faculty! In form and moving, how express and admirable! In action how like an angel, in apprehension how like a god! The beauty of the world. The paragon of animals." (II.ii.293–297)

Hamlet praises our ability to understand and interpret the world around us. However, the play is full of ambiguities that neither Hamlet nor the audience can solve. The world of Hamlet is a world of uncertainties.

List as many of the play's uncertainties as possible. Consider supernatural and metaphysical matters, as well as issues of guilt and innocence, motivation or behavior, feelings, and degrees of sanity or insanity. What can we know in a play so full of unknowns?

And the Oscar Goes to....

Playing Hamlet is often considered to be the pinnacle of an actor's career, and everyone from Mel Gibson and Ethan Hawke to Laurence Olivier and Sarah Bernhardt has played the mad prince of Denmark. What characteristics do you think make for a good Hamlet? Of all the actors working today, who do you think would make the best Hamlet? Write a paragraph about who'd be best—and why.

Vexing Gertrude

Furious with his mother, Hamlet condemns her in Act I, saying:

> "Frailty, thy name is woman!" (I.ii.146)

Why is Hamlet so angry with Gertrude? Does she merit his scorn? Write a paragraph about what makes Gertrude a particularly exasperating, hard-to-understand character. Be specific.

The Biggest Question

In his most famous **soliloquy**—a speech delivered alone onstage—Hamlet contemplates suicide:

> "To be, or not to be: that is the question:
> Whether 'tis nobler in the mind to suffer
> The slings and arrows of outrageous fortune,
> Or to take arms against a sea of troubles,
> And by opposing end them? To die: to sleep;
> No more; and by a sleep to say we end
> The heart-ache and the thousand natural shocks
> That flesh is heir to, 'tis a consummation
> Devoutly to be wish'd. To die, to sleep;
> To sleep: perchance to dream: ay, there's the rub." (III.i.57–66)

How does Hamlet imagine death? Why might we be scared of death, according to Hamlet? Explain your thoughts in a paragraph.

Does Father Know Best?

In Act I, Polonius gives Laertes a speech full of clichéd fatherly advice, including:

"Give every man thy ear but few thy voice.
Take each man's censure but reserve thy judgment.
Costly thy habit as thy purse can buy,
But not expressed in fancy—rich, not gaudy,
For the apparel oft proclaims the man." (I.iii.68–72)

Make a list of advice that you have heard from older relatives. Then reread Polonius's speech. How does your list resemble Polonius's speech? How does it differ? Which pieces of advice are worth heeding?

Friend or Foil?

Various characters in this play seem to be **foils** for Hamlet—that is, the characters' personalities or behavior contrast with and accentuate those of Hamlet.

Choose one male character and discuss how he differs from Hamlet. In what ways is he similar to Hamlet? How does he function as Hamlet's foil? What does he show or tell us about Hamlet?

To Be, or Not

Upon leaving a performance of *Hamlet*, a man turns to his wife and says, "That play was full of famous quotes." What's your favorite famous Hamlet quote? Why?

The Lunatic Actor, the Acting Lunatic

Is Hamlet faking madness, or is he really insane? Throughout the play, Hamlet pretends that he has gone mad, but his behavior becomes increasingly unpredictable. What do you think? Use specific quotes from the play to support your position.

About Ophelia....

Ophelia, a beautiful young woman, goes insane after Hamlet rejects her and murders her father, Polonius. Eventually, Ophelia drowns herself, but not before lecturing about the exploitative nature of young men. She sings:

> "Young men will do't, if they come to 't.
>   By Cock, they are to blame.
> Quoth she, 'Before you tumbled me,
>   You promised me to wed.'
> He answers,
> 'So would I ha'done, by yonder sun,
>   An thou hadst not come to my bed.' " (IV.v.59–65)

Write a paragraph about Ophelia's role in the play. Does Hamlet love her? Has he stopped loving her? What's her relationship to the other men in her life? Why does she kill herself?

90

Outrageous Outrage

Before departing the oppressive world of her Aunt Reed's home, Jane Eyre verbally assaults her aunt. She rants:

> "I am glad you are no relation of mine. I will never call you aunt again as long as I live. I will never come to visit you when I am grown up; and if any one asks me how I liked you, and how you treated me, I will say the very thought of you makes me sick, and that you treated me with miserable cruelty." (Chapter 4)

Have you ever had an experience like this? Were your circumstances truly as awful as Jane's, or did it just seem that way at the time? Write a paragraph about a time when you felt angry enough to make comments like this toward someone.

Eyre and Burns

Jane Eyre and Helen Burns become close friends at Lowood School, bonded by shared circumstances.

How are Jane and Helen similar? How are they different? Make a list of their similarities and differences, using examples from the novel.

93

DAILY SPARK

GREAT BOOKS

Jane Eyre

The Perfect Love

Jane Eyre spends much of the novel searching for a love that neither forces her to sacrifice her identity nor harms her autonomy in any way.

Was her goal realistic in the nineteenth century? Is it a realistic goal now? Explain why or why not in a paragraph.

Revolutionary Jane

At the time of the novel's publication, Jane Eyre's views concerning religion, class, and gender were considered radical.

Think about how times have changed. Have things changed that much?

What are some revolutionary views in today's world? If *Jane Eyre* were updated to the twenty-first century, who would Jane be and what would her radical views deal with? Write a paragraph about this twenty-first-century Jane.

Jane Eyre

The Madwoman in the Attic

Critics have interpreted Bertha Mason as a symbol: some say Bertha stands for the other cultures the British Empire encountered and colonized, but feared and "locked away." Others suggest that Bertha typifies the trapped Victorian wife, who lacked outlets for her creativity, ideas, and frustration due to the limits placed upon her by society and marriage.

Which of these theories about Bertha strikes you as plausible, given your interpretation of the novel? Or do you have another theory? Explain your views in a paragraph or two.

Jane Eyre as Social Criticism

Jane Eyre has an extremely ambiguous position in society. As a governess, she is the intellectual equal of a powerful man like Rochester. Yet, at the same time, she is a servant who will never be his social equal.

How does the novel criticize the social prejudices and hypocrisies of Victorian society? You might first identify the various prejudices under discussion, then find examples of how characters behave when confronted with those prejudices and hypocrisies. Write a paragraph summarizing your findings.

"Too Absolute a Stagnation"

Jane Eyre overtly takes issue with the conditions of Victorian women. She protests:

> Women are supposed to be very calm generally: but women feel just as men feel; they need exercise for their faculties and a field for their efforts as much as their brothers do; they suffer from too rigid a restraint, too absolute a stagnation, precisely as men would suffer; and it is narrow-minded in their more privileged fellow-creatures to say that they ought to confine themselves to making puddings and knitting stockings, to playing on the piano and embroidering bags. It is thoughtless to condemn them, or laugh at them, if they seek to do more or learn more than custom has pronounced necessary for their sex. (Chapter 12)

Clearly Jane feels imprisoned by society's expectation of women. Think of examples of other characters in stories or of groups in history who share or have shared similar feelings. List them. What have these individuals or groups done to overcome society's chains?

Should She Stay, or Should She Go?

At the end of Chapter 27, Jane Eyre feels torn between her desire to stay with Rochester and her need to preserve her moral integrity. Although she loves him and knows he is the only person who has ever truly loved her, she also knows that staying would mean compromising herself by becoming his mistress, since he remains married to Bertha Mason.

Ultimately, Jane chooses to leave Rochester.

What choice would you make in a similar position? Write a paragraph about what you would do—and why.

Jane Eyre

Jane's Happy/Unhappy Ending

The following passage from the novel's happy ending is highly controversial:

> I have now been married ten years. I know what it is to live entirely for and with what I love best on earth. I hold myself supremely blest—blest beyond what language can express; because I am my husband's life as fully as he is mine ... I know no weariness of my Edward's society: he knows none of mine ... consequently, we are ever together. To be together is for us to be at once as free as in solitude, as gay as in company. We talk, I believe, all day long; to talk to each other is but a more animated and an audible thinking. All my confidence is bestowed on him, all his confidence is devoted to me; we are precisely suited in character—perfect concord is the result.

Some critics argue that Charlotte Brontë has allowed Jane Eyre to sacrifice her precious autonomy and merge with Rochester, becoming the same passive Victorian woman both Brontë and Jane seem to criticize. Other critics argue that Jane has found the love she sought all along, suggesting that Rochester allows Jane to be herself.

What do you think? Organize your thoughts into a paragraph.

Hail Brutus

Many readers see Brutus as the tragic hero of this play: they cite his inflexible sense of honor and devotion to the Republic of Rome as his **tragic flaw**—the failing in a person's character that brings about his or her ruin. Brutus's internal conflicts drive the action of the second half of the play.

Does the extreme sense of honor that Brutus possesses seem realistic to you? Is he the play's true hero? Why or why not? Write a paragraph about Brutus.

Jealous Cassius

Cassius is a talented general with power in his own right. However, he is unhappy that the Romans have elevated Julius Caesar to the status of a god.

Write a paragraph in which you compare Cassius to other jealous, conniving characters that you have read about or seen on film. How is he like them? How is he unique? Be specific.

The Personal and the Political

In *Julius Caesar*, things go wrong, in part because characters have trouble balancing their public and private lives. Brutus neglects his private feelings and focuses only on what he thinks is the public good. Julius Caesar tells Mark Antony that he can't trust Cassius, because Cassius has no private life and his character consists solely of ambition. Other characters confuse their public and private selves.

Is it ever wise to mix business and pleasure? If so, when? Drawing your examples from contemporary life, write a paragraph about some people who have successfully balanced their public and private lives and some people who have confused the two. What happened in each instance?

Steadfast Caesar

Just prior to his assassination, Julius Caesar gives a speech in which he praises himself and discusses his constancy and unwillingness to change his mind:

"I could be well moved if I were as you.
   If I could pray to move, prayers would move me.
   But I am as constant as the Northern Star,
   Of whose true fixed and resting quality
   There is no fellow in the firmament.
   The skies are painted with unnumbered sparks;
   They are all fire, and every one doth shine;
   But there's but one in all doth hold his place." (III.i.58–65)

Does anyone you know have such a high opinion of himself or herself? Who is this person? From your point of view, is that person's self-opinion deserved? In what ways is this person similar to and different from Caesar? Write a paragraph about this person.

"Friends, Romans, Countrymen"

Brutus foolishly allows Mark Antony to make a speech at Julius Caesar's funeral. Antony gives a funeral oration for Caesar and turns public opinion against the conspirators. An excerpt:

> "Come I to speak in Caesar's funeral.
> He was my friend, faithful and just to me:
> But Brutus says he was ambitious;
> And Brutus is an honourable man.
> He hath brought many captives home to Rome,
> Whose ransoms did the general coffers fill:
> Did this in Caesar seem ambitious?
> When that the poor have cried, Caesar hath wept:
> Ambition should be made of sterner stuff:
> Yet Brutus says he was ambitious;
> And Brutus is an honorable man." (III.ii.82–92)

How does Antony influence the crowd? Discuss how Antony sways the mourners over to his side with his rhetorical skill. Specifically, what in this speech is so convincing?

Now or Never

Brutus attempts to sway Cassius and persuade him to battle Octavius and Antony:

"Under your pardon. You must note besides,
That we have tried the utmost of our friends,
Our legions are brim-full, our cause is ripe:
The enemy increaseth every day;
We, at the height, are ready to decline.
There is a tide in the affairs of men
Which, taken at the flood, leads on to fortune;
Omitted, all the voyage of their life
Is bound in shallows and in miseries.
On such a full sea are we now afloat;
And we must take the current when it serves,
Or lose our ventures." (IV.iii.216–227)

What do you think? Is there a right time for action? Do free will and fate hinge upon each other? If so, how? Write a paragraph in which you agree or disagree with Brutus.

Republic of Superstition

Throughout *Julius Caesar*, characters pay attention to omens, using them to establish their fates and courses of action.

Make a list of omens in this play. How do the different characters read them? What conclusions can you make about the omens? Do the omens have any impact on the action of the play?

And I Quote....

Today's politicians still love to take quotations about statehood, leadership, conspiracy, assassination, and war from *Julius Caesar.*

Imagine that you are running for office. What scenes or speeches from this play would you quote? Why?

DAILY SPARK

GREAT BOOKS

Friendship, Enemyship

Julius Caesar portrays a man who helps kill his best friend. The play can thus be read as a study of friends and enemies.

Look at any pairing of so-called friends in *Julius Caesar*. Write a paragraph about how they relate with and talk about one another. Are these true friends? Would you want friends like this? Why or why not?

Fascinating Island

Many books, television shows, and movies take life on a desert island as their central plot. Why? What makes marooned characters so fascinating?

Write a paragraph about a few books, shows, or movies that feature marooned characters struggling against the landscape or against one another. What do these characters have in common? Why is life on a desert island such an oft-employed plot?

Casting the Castaways

You, a high-powered movie mogul, have just purchased the rights to William Golding's novel. **Which actors will you choose to play the parts of Ralph, Piggy, Jack, Simon, Roger, Sam, and Eric?** Why might you favor one actor over another for a particular role?

Lord of the Flies

This Equals That

Lord of the Flies is an **allegory**—that is, the characters and objects in the novel stand for significant ideas, themes, and abstractions.

Make a list of the characters and objects that you believe represent ideas, themes, or abstractions. Indicate what you think each character or object you list might stand for.

The Good, the Bad, the Island

In his novel, William Golding creates a world in which evil dominates human nature. In the end, the evil in the boys overpowers the good.

Write a paragraph about what you think: do you believe that the island world created by Golding is a microcosm of our larger society? Are people inherently evil? If left unchecked, will evil always rule?

The Suffering of Swine

Piggy, perhaps the smartest of the boys, suffers the most abuse. The other boys pick on him, harass him, or simply ignore him. Why? How does Piggy fit in with the rest of the story? Write a paragraph about what the character of Piggy might stand for or represent.

Special Simon

William Golding depicts Simon as being much different from the rest of the boys on the island. Write a paragraph about what makes Simon unique. Do you know any real-life Simons? What makes them so special?

The Sixty-Year-Old Beast

At two separate moments in the novel, Simon explains that the beast is within us. Some critics attribute William Golding's vision of evil to his experiences in World War II. If Golding were writing today, do you think he would have the same view of humanity? Have humans become more evil since World War II, or have the last sixty or so years made us better people? Write a paragraph or two in which you discuss your views.

Jack's Inner Drive

His mind was crowded with memories; memories of the knowledge that had come to them when they closed in on the struggling pig, knowledge that they had outwitted a living thing, imposed their will upon it, taken away its life like a long satisfying drink. (Chapter 4)

After Jack kills his first pig, he is overwhelmed by excitement and joy.

Write a paragraph about what Jack's state of mind at this moment, as revealed by this passage, suggests about his character and inner motivations.

The End of Innocence

The narrator explains Ralph's reaction upon the realization that he is no longer a child:

> Ralph wept for the end of innocence, the darkness of man's heart, and the fall through the air of a true, wise friend called Piggy. (Chapter 12)

Write a paragraph about a time when you realized that you were no longer an innocent child. Was this a moment of despair for you, as it was for Ralph, or was it a moment of joy? Explain.

The Cover-Up Cycle

The action of this play centers around a king and his queen covering up their dirty deeds to maintain their power.

Make a list of Macbeth's actions and reactions. How does one dirty deed lead to another?

Macbeth

The Making of a Monarch

Shakespeare wrote *Macbeth* as a tribute to King James I of England. Upon her death, Queen Elizabeth named James, then king of Scotland, as her successor. James ruled England and Scotland, veritable enemies, from 1603 to 1625. As a compliment to him, the play deals, in part, with the ideas of political legitimacy and of moral authority.

When, where, and how does the play suggest that Macbeth has political legitimacy to rule as king? What about moral authority to rule? Of all the characters, which ruler seems to have the most right, political or otherwise, to the throne? Explain your views in a paragraph or two.

To See Without Seeing

After Macbeth kills King Duncan, guilt and paranoia overwhelm him. Frightened and alone, he begins his soliloquy:

"Is this a dagger which I see before me,
  The handle toward my hand? Come, let me clutch thee.
  I have thee not, and yet I see thee still.
  Art thou not, fatal vision, sensible
  To feeling as to sight? or art thou but
  A dagger of the mind, a false creation,
  Proceeding from the heat-oppressed brain?
  I see thee yet....
  Mine eyes are made the fools o'the other senses,
  Or else worth all the rest: I see thee still;
  And on thy blade and dudgeon gouts of blood,
  Which was not so before." (II.i.33–47)

How does Shakespeare emphasize Macbeth's feelings in this soliloquy? Make a list of the literary devices or rhetorical techniques that are employed.

Lady Macbeth

Of the female characters in Shakespeare, Lady Macbeth is perhaps the most complicated. What do you think of her? Do you feel sympathy toward her? Does she possess worthy or likable qualities? Why or why not? Write a paragraph about Lady M.

Ambition and Power

Most readers blame Macbeth's downfall on an excess of ambition. What do you think?

Write a short outline of a screenplay that features an excessively ambitious character. What happens to your hero once he or she gets a taste of power?

Macbeth

The Play's So Popular

What makes *Macbeth* so popular? The violence? The psychological, psychotic motivation? The weird witches? Write a paragraph about why people love this play.

Wracked with Guilt

Guilt produces particularly awful results in *Macbeth*. Write a paragraph in which you discuss how guilt torments both Macbeth and Lady Macbeth. Be specific. Do you think Shakespeare realistically portrays their suffering? Why or why not?

Macbeth's Men and Women

Macbeth discusses gender and gender roles, particularly in relation to Macbeth and Lady Macbeth. Make a list of the play's references to masculinity and femininity. For each example, discuss what masculinity or femininity is supposed to "mean." What does the play have to say about life as a man and life as a woman?

Opposing Opposites

Throughout *Macbeth,* Shakespeare pairs opposites in order to play with our understanding of the natural or just order of the universe. He contrasts men and women, fairness and foulness, natural and unnatural, and morality and immorality.

Try to find as many examples of paired opposites as you can. Then discuss what each example demonstrates about its opposite.

Of Mice and Men

Flat or Fleshy?

Some readers criticize *Of Mice and Men* for having two-dimensional characters. What do you think? Does this criticism have merit? Do the characters seem real, or are they "flat"—that is, lacking in complexity and depth? Why or why not? Write a paragraph about your thoughts.

Curley's Wife

Of Mice and Men has only one female character, and she has no name. She is simply known as "Curley's wife." The men on the farm call her a "tart" and a "tramp," because her sexuality tempts them.

Write a paragraph about Curley's wife. Is she a villain, or is she a victim like all of the other characters?

© 2006 SparkNotes LLC

Of Mice and Men

Protecting the Innocent

George goes out of his way to protect Lennie, his slow-witted, lumbering giant of a friend, from people. To George, people and their institutions cannot understand Lennie, and they can only hurt him.

Have you ever felt so protective of a friend or family member? How did you protect that person? Explain what happened in a paragraph or two.

John Steinbeck and the American Dream

Like many American authors, including F. Scott Fitzgerald, John Steinbeck skewers the American Dream. Steinbeck suggests that the freedom to follow one's own desires is impossible.

Make a list of all the characters in the novel. What do you learn about each character that suggests that he or she will never be able to fulfill his or her dream?

The Power of Friendship

Throughout the work of John Steinbeck, the power of friendship emerges as an important theme. An underlying belief that relationships can transform our lives and make suffering bearable appears in *Of Mice and Men*, as when George explains his relationship with Lennie:

> "Guys like us, that work on ranches, are the loneliest guys in the world. They got no family. They don't belong no place…. With us it ain't like that. We got a future. We got somebody to talk to that gives a damn about us. We don't have to sit in no bar room blowin' in our jack jus' because we got no place else to go. If them other guys gets in jail they can rot for all anybody gives a damn. But not us." (Section 1)

Write a paragraph about what sets Lennie and George apart from other guys. What keeps them going?

Crooks on Life

After Lennie shares with Crooks his plan to buy a farm, Crooks tries to spoil Lennie's hopes. He tells Lennie:

"I seen hundreds of men come by on the road an' on the ranches, with their bindles on their back an' that same damn thing in their heads ... every damn one of 'em's got a little piece of land in his head. An' never a God damn one of 'em ever gets it. Just like heaven. Ever'body wants a little piece of lan'. I read plenty of books out here. Nobody never gets to heaven, and nobody gets no land." (Section 4)

What do Crooks's comments indicate about his character or personality? What do they say about human nature? Organize your thoughts into a paragraph.

Of Mice and Men

Steinbeck and Nature

John Steinbeck often draws his imagery from nature. Pick a passage from *Of Mice and Men* in which Steinbeck describes a scene from the natural world. Then write a paragraph or two about how the passage illustrates Steinbeck's attitude toward nature, as well as nature's role in the novel.

Lights, Camera, Steinbeck

Agree or disagree? There's something cinematic about *Of Mice and Men*. Consider the structure and language of Steinbeck's novel. What about them makes the novel seem so much like a movie? Organize your thoughts and examples into a paragraph.

A Poet Is Born

Of Mice and Men contains some lovely, poetic moments. One way to appreciate their poetic qualities is to transform them into poetry.

Pick a section of at least eight lines from the novel. Next, remove any little or meaningless words from the passage, including *the, an*, and *or*. Manipulate the lines of the passage, adding line breaks and deleting punctuation as necessary. Finally, add a title to your poem.

Love and Violence

The love affair between Romeo and Juliet leads to fighting, bloodshed, threats of suicide, and actual suicides.

Make a list of other movies or books that link passionate love to ultra-violence. Are violence and love commonly linked, or is Shakespeare's play thematically unique?

Romeo and Juliet

Unfrocking the Friar

The advice, action, and schemes of Friar Lawrence help motivate and move the events of *Romeo and Juliet*. But his behavior and knowledge don't seem to fit in with the typical Catholic friar.

Write a paragraph about the discrepancy between Friar Lawrence and a typical Catholic friar or priest. In what ways is Friar Lawrence a characteristic man of the cloth, and in what ways is he unique? Be specific in your examples.

Everything in Moderation

Romeo, a passionate young man, tends to act hastily and rashly. Friar Lawrence advises him to behave more moderately, less quickly and extremely, to avoid danger and mistakes. Yet Romeo does not listen.

Why does Romeo ignore the friar's advice? Is Romeo a realistic representation of a passionate young man, or is he too extreme in his hot-headedness? Do you know anyone in real life who behaves similarly to Romeo? Explain.

Darkness and Light

More light and light, more dark and dark our woes. (III.v.36)

Throughout the play, Shakespeare uses imagery of light and darkness in various ways, without any fixed or consistent meaning. Light is not necessarily good, and dark is not necessarily bad.

Pick one scene in the play and note any language that deals with light and darkness. For each image of light or darkness, assess the image for its positive or negative sense. When is light bright and darkness dark? When is light dark and darkness light?

139

DAILY SPARK

GREAT BOOKS

Four Days

The events in *Romeo and Juliet* seem to occur at an extraordinary pace. Everything happens over only four days—a possibility or an impossibility in the real world?

How does Shakespeare achieve the effect of acceleration during the course of the play? Make a list of literary devices and rhetorical techniques used in *Romeo and Juliet.*

Romeo and Juliet

Memorable Mercutio

One of Shakespeare's most memorable characters, Mercutio, says extraordinary things, clashes with Tybalt, creates comic relief, and speaks the glorious Queen Mab speech. He is, in effect, a remarkable supporting character. Right?

Or is he more than a supporting character? Does Mercutio have a serious role in the play, or did Shakespeare include him only for fun? What do you think? Use specific details to support your answer.

Everyone's a Critic

Within the grandiose drama about star-crossed lovers and feuding families comes some sharp social commentary. *Romeo and Juliet* is about more than the noble characters and their dramatic, tragic storylines: it also portrays the difficulties of the lower classes, who cannot afford to be melodramatic as they battle disease and poverty.

Focus on one of the lower-class or servant characters in the play, such as the nurse, Peter, the apothecary, or the musicians. Reread sections involving this character and write a paragraph about exactly how, in simple ways, this character suffers. What kind of social criticism might this character be enacting or dramatizing?

Queen Mab Is Fab

In Act I, Mercutio tells Romeo that Romeo has been visited by Queen Mab. An excerpt from his playful, fun speech:

"[Queen Mab] is the fairies' midwife; and she comes
In shape no bigger than an agate-stone ...
Drawn with a team of little atomies
Athwart men's noses as they lie asleep:
Her waggon-spokes made of long spinners' legs;
The cover, of the wings of grasshoppers;
The traces, of the smallest spider's web;
The collars, of the moonshine's watery beams;
Her whip, of cricket's bone; the lash, of film;
Her waggoner, a small grey-coated gnat." (I.iv.56–65)

Mercutio describes Queen Mab as the midwife of the fairies, a creature no bigger than a finger. What are some of the queen's other characteristics, according to Mercutio?
Put Mercutio's speech into your own words, using modern English.

720 Minutes to Love

Romeo and Juliet meet at the Capulets' party, then speak briefly later. By the end of the night, they are married. Do you think it's possible to fall in love in less than twelve hours? Why or why not? Write a paragraph in which you defend your views.

A Tale of Two Cities

It Was the Best of Times....

The opening lines of *A Tale of Two Cites* are some of the most famous in all of Western literature:

> It was the best of times, it was the worst of times, it was the age of wisdom, it was the age of foolishness, it was the epoch of belief, it was the epoch of incredulity, it was the season of Light, it was the season of Darkness, it was the spring of hope, it was the winter of despair, we had everything before us, we had nothing before us, we were all going direct to Heaven, we were all going direct the other way....

Based on these lines alone, what sorts of events, characters, and plot might you expect from this novel? Why? Make a list or write a paragraph summarizing your views.

Who Are You Calling Flat?

Some scholars criticize Charles Dickins for creating "flat" characters—characters that lack complexity or depth.

Write a paragraph in which you agree or disagree with this criticism. Does Lucie Manette seem too sweet to believe? Is Madame Defarge a bit too evil to be real? Why or why not?

Tune in Next Week....

A Tale of Two Cities was published as a serial novel, in weekly installments, from April 20 to November 26, 1859. Its structure and style—including short chapters and specific subheadings—were intended to keep readers freshly involved in the plot, constantly craving more, and willing to wait for the next installment. Charles Dickens aimed to create a popular novel, and he created lots of suspense early on in the story to make sure that his novel was marketable.

If this novel were a modern-day television series, would it be popular? Why or why not? If not, discuss what changes would have to be made in order for this story to suit twenty-first-century tastes.

What's Your Secret?

Early in the novel, the narrator establishes an important theme—the inability of people to really know one another:

> A wonderful fact to reflect upon, that every human creature is constituted to be that profound secret and mystery to every other. A solemn consideration, when I enter a great city by night, that every one of those darkly clustered houses encloses its own secret; that every room in every one of them encloses its own secret; that every beating heart in the hundreds of thousands of breasts there is, in some of its imaginings, a secret to the heart nearest it! (Book I, Chapter 3)

Do you think your friends know everything about you? Do you think that people can truly be known and understood by others? Write a paragraph discussing your views.

A Tale of Two Cities

How About Those Revolutionaries?

Charles Dickens can be fairly heavy-handed in his portrayal of the French peasants during the Revolution. They spill wine in the streets and do other unruly things. They also imprison and execute innocents, such as Charles Darnay, for the crimes of ancestors.

What do you make of Dickens's portrayal of the peasants? Is it a sympathetic portrayal? Or is the portrayal more complicated than sheer sympathy? Write a paragraph discussing your views.

Condemned!

The revolutionaries seem to go too far in their quest to end suffering and transform their unjust world. Determined to cleanse France of the evils of the exploitative aristocracy, they appear to be out for the blood of *anyone* of noble descent.

Imagine that you, like Charles Darnay, are sentenced to death for the crimes of your ancestors. Write a paragraph about how you would respond. Are there ever circumstances in which people should pay for the actions of their ancestors? Explain.

Perform It!

A Tale of Two Cities contains a number of dramatic scenes. Characters reveal shocking secrets about themselves, and their lives and fates are changed in a matter of mere seconds.

Choose your favorite dramatic moment in the novel. Working by yourself or with a partner, transform your moment into a scene from a play. Add stage directions and modify dialogue as necessary, and carefully consider any costumes your characters should wear.

"A Far, Far Better Thing"

Sydney Carton sacrifices his life so that his beloved Lucie Manette and her family can enjoy a happy life together.

Does this ending work for you? Do you find the romance of it appealing, or is it too far-fetched? Can you imagine a real-life situation in which you or someone you know would choose to die for another? Organize your thoughts into a paragraph.

One Is Good, Two Is Better

Many critics have noted that the characters in *A Tale of Two Cities* are doubled—that is, characters seem to be paired or to have opposites. For example, Miss Pross connects to Madame Defarge, while Sydney Carton aligns with Charles Darnay.

Pick one character pair and discuss the characters' similarities, differences, and relationship to each other in a paragraph.

GREAT

Scout's P.O.V.

In Harper Lee's novel, Scout tells the story in retrospect, as an adult. Yet Lee allows the point of view to fluctuate: at times, Scout gives a child's understanding of events, but elsewhere the perspective is decidedly mature and adult.

What's the effect of these shifts? To generate your answer, consider comparing two scenes, one from the point of view of the child Scout and one from the point of view of the adult Scout.

Good Teaching?

To Kill a Mockingbird includes a number of characters who serve as teachers of one kind or another. Interestingly, Miss Caroline, the one character who is a teacher by profession, seems to have a great deal of difficulty understanding her students and what they need from her.

Which characters are good teachers? What makes them good teachers? Write a paragraph in which you compare them to Miss Caroline: how do they succeed where she fails?

Three Cheers for Atticus

Atticus Finch is an excellent role model for his kids in a number of ways. Although he's not always home and doesn't do things the way some "respectable" parents in Maycomb County do, he allows his kids to think for themselves, sticks to his morals regardless of public opinion, and shows everyone how all people deserve to be treated.

Does Atticus seem real to you? Why or why not? If not, does he seem like an ideal to which we should aspire? In a novel filled with damaged, twisted adults, how does Atticus maintain his strength and his sanity? Write a paragraph summarizing your thoughts about Atticus.

To Kill a Mockingbird

Empathy as Skin

Atticus gives Scout some simple moral advice, which seems to help her develop empathy:

"You never really understand a person until you consider things from his point of view ... until you climb into his skin and walk around in it." (Chapter 3)

Have you ever tried to climb into someone else's skin? Whose? How did it feel to see the world from that person's eyes? Alternatively, is there someone whom you cannot understand—at least not yet—because you are not able to slip into his or her skin? Explain yourself in a paragraph.

Maycomb's Elaborate Social System

Harper Lee deals with race and class throughout *To Kill a Mockingbird*. She creates a complicated social hierarchy in Maycomb County that reflects the social hierarchy that existed in small towns across the South.

Chart out the social hierarchy in Maycomb County, from top to bottom. Which groups or types of people have the most power? Which have the least? Which characters belong to which group?

To Kill a....

"Remember it's a sin to kill a mockingbird." That was the only time I ever heard Atticus say it was a sin to do something, and I asked Miss Maudie about it.

"Your father's right," she said. "Mockingbirds don't do one thing but make music for us to enjoy ... but sing their hearts out for us. That's why it's a sin to kill a mockingbird." (Chapter 10)

Based on Miss Maudie's above explanation to Scout's question, which characters in the novel are mockingbirds? What's the relationship between these characters and the title of the novel? Do you think the novel's title works, or do you think Harper Lee should have chosen another word or phrase? Explain.

DAILY SPARK

GREAT BOOKS

© 2006 SparkNotes LLC

An Ideal Character

Critics have observed that the black community in Maycomb seems to be idealized—that is, it seems to be almost perfect and not at all realistic. These critics argue that Harper Lee emphasizes the positive characteristics of Calpurnia, Tom Robinson, and the other black characters, but doesn't point out any negative qualities they might have.

What do you think? Are the black characters idealized? Why or why not? Are any of the white characters idealized? If so, who? If not, why not? Write a paragraph outlining your views.

To Kill a Mockingbird

Twenty-First-Century Maycomb

Harper Lee sets *To Kill a Mockingbird* during the Great Depression. Imagine that you could choose a new setting for the novel. Which historical era would you choose, and why? How would the novel's mood, themes, and events change, based on its new setting? Write a paragraph discussing the effects of your new setting.

Ahoy, Adulthood

At its heart, *To Kill a Mockingbird* is a coming-of-age story, especially for Jem, but also for Scout.

Write about your own "coming of age" experience(s). Compare yourself to Jem or Scout: whose experience of the complicated adult world has been more difficult? Why? How?

The Iliad

Achilles? A Hero?

Much of *The Iliad* centers on the character of Achilles. Homer gives Achilles a number of serious character flaws, particularly a focus on petty concerns. Still, the ancient Greeks viewed Achilles as extremely heroic.

Based on your reading of the poem, which qualities would make Achilles a hero to the ancient Greeks? What about today? In our world, do you think people would view him as a hero? Write a paragraph explaining why or why not.

Choosing *Kleos*

In situation after situation, Homer forces his characters to choose between their loved ones and the quest for *kleos*, or heroic glory. The most heroic characters—that is, the ones the Ancient Greeks would like best—seem always to choose *kleos* over loved ones. Characters like Paris, who choose to spend time with loved ones rather than fight, are mocked.

Do people of today value *kleos* over love? Write a paragraph about how society regards individuals who choose glory over love. Are they respected? Why or why not? Be sure to back up your views with examples.

The Iliad

Picking Favorites

In *The Iliad,* a god's kindness toward one mortal often means harm to another mortal or even another god, a fact that saddens Ares:

> "We everlasting gods … ah what chilling blows
> We suffer—thanks to our own conflicting wills—
> Whenever we show these mortal men some kindness." (Book 5)

Does favoritism always harm some people? Does an employer's support of one employee damage another employee? Can parents' favoritism of one child hurt the other—or even hurt the parents? Explain.

Woe Are Humans

Zeus suggests that humans suffer more cruelly at the hands of the gods than any other animal:

"There is nothing alive more agonized than man
of all that breathe and crawl across the earth." (Book 17)

In the eyes of Zeus, what particular quality causes humans to suffer more than other creatures? Refer to Book 17 as you're writing your paragraph. Is Zeus right? Why or why not?

Marching Knowingly to Their Dooms

Homer gives his heroes, such as Achilles and Hector, prior knowledge of their fates, thereby making them more heroic for choosing to die. They are not ignorant of their future; rather, they go to their dooms because they must.

What do you think? Does this foreknowledge of their fates make the heroes more heroic—or more robotic? Explain your views in a paragraph or two.

A Hero Is Not a Grinder

Think fast: what does the word *hero* mean to you? How might Homer define *hero*, based on your understanding of *The Iliad*? Are the definitions very similar or vastly different?

Fathers and Sons

The Iliad focuses largely on the relationships between fathers and sons—between Priam and Hector, between Achilles and Peleus, and so on. Choose one of the father-son relationships in the epic. Discuss how this relationship works. Is it healthy? Is it realistic? Does it resemble any real-life relationships you've seen? Why or why not?

Holy Comic Relief

The gods in *The Iliad* often provide comic relief. Find three examples of how the gods bring humor to an otherwise dark work. How does the humor come out? What makes the scenes or moments funny?

The Iliad

Honorably, Nobly, Wisely, Bravely

The Iliad emphasizes the fleeting nature of human life. Throughout his epic, Homer implies that only words and deeds survive: to be remembered, we should live nobly and wisely.

What do you think? To be remembered after death, how should a person live? Should a person focus on creating a lasting reputation? If so, how? If not, why not? How do you plan to live?

Structurally Elaborate

The Odyssey has an elaborate structure: the epic features both numerous flashbacks to Odysseus's adventures and subplots that star Odysseus's son Telemachus and his wife, Penelope.

How do the epic's different storylines and episodes enrich the reading experience? How do they make the act of reading more challenging? Write a paragraph explaining your views.

From Child to Man-Child to Man

Much of *The Odyssey* focuses on the initiation of Telemachus, Odysseus's son, into adulthood. Think about what sorts of rituals Telemachus must perform and what sorts of behaviors or adventures he must undertake.

Does contemporary society contain any initiation rituals? Provide an example of how one culture in our society marks the transition from child or young adult into mature adult. Does the initiation differ for men and women or from culture to culture? If so, how?

The Triumph of Brawny Wit

Whereas *The Iliad* concerns itself with physical strength and heroic deeds in war, *The Odyssey* deals more with wits and cunning. In fact, Homer repeatedly emphasizes Odysseus's clever mind, showing how it makes Odysseus superior to others.

List five examples from *The Odyssey* in which intelligence triumphs over physical strength.

Tempting, Isn't It?

Odysseus and his crew want to make it home, yet various temptations continually arise and attempt to sway them from their course.

Describe a time in which you had several temptations or distractions attempting to thwart your pursuit of a goal. What were the temptations, distractions, and goal(s)? Were you thwarted? If so, how? If not, how did you overcome those temptations and distractions?

Playing Dress Up

Throughout *The Odyssey,* characters—from the goddess Athena to Odysseus himself—disguise themselves. Disguise helps characters evade capture. When Odysseus arrives home, disguise enables him to identify which characters truly love him, as only those characters are able to see through his disguise.

Think about other books or movies that feature characters playing dress up. Write a paragraph about how a disguise helps a character reveal or hide something.

Odysseus and Achilles Chat

Odysseus visits the underworld and has a meaningful conversation with the deceased hero Achilles:

> "But you, Achilles,
>   there's not a man in the world more blest than you …
>   Time was, when you were alive, we Argives
>   honored you as a god, and now down here, I see,
>   you lord it over the dead in all your power.
>   So grieve no more at dying, Great Achilles."
> I reassured the ghost, but he broke out, protesting,
> "No winning words about death to me, shining Odysseus!
> By god, I'd rather slave on earth for another man—
>   some dirt-poor tenant farmer who scrapes to keep alive—
>   than rule down here over all the breathless dead." (Book 11)

What does Achilles try to impart to Odysseus and to us? Do you agree? Respond to the exchange between the two heroes.

Woman and *The Odyssey*

Women seem to have strange and contradictory roles in *The Odyssey*. Odysseus's wife, Penelope, for example, is a complicated character. She has not seen her husband, whom she loves deeply, for twenty years. In his absence, she entertains numerous suitors, and she never refuses to marry—she only puts off making a decision.

What do you think the role of women is in this epic? How do you think Homer portrays them? Compare the various female characters in order to construct a short argument about women and *The Odyssey*.

GREAT BOOKS

Today's Odyssey

This epic contains any number of magical, comical, and dramatic events. For instance, the crew opens a leather bag and unleashes a hurricane, the witch Circe turns men into pigs, and Penelope constructs elaborate games for her suitors, among other situations. Which event from the entire epic is your favorite?

Update your favorite event to take place in the twenty-first century. Take as much poetic and dramatic license as necessary, making sure that you account for contemporary fashions, attitudes, behaviors, and language.

I, Value

Homer's readers would have responded wholeheartedly to the distinct body of ideas and values portrayed in *The Odyssey*. For example, there was the value of *kleos*, or honor, that would have been essential to the life of a hero, such as Odysseus. There was also the important value of *xenia*, a combination of generosity, good manners, and hospitality.

Make a list of Homeric values that you encountered in your reading. Indicate which values you believe make up a large part of your life today and write about the place that these values hold in your life.